THE JOURNEY

THE JOURNEY

THE INSPIRATION AND MESSAGE BEHIND THE MUSIC

ROSETTA PERRY

Copyright © 2021 J Merrill Publishing, Inc.

All rights reserved. No part of this publication may be reproduced, distributed, or transmitted in any form or by any means, including photocopying, recording, or other electronic or mechanical methods, without the prior written permission of the publisher, except in the case of brief quotations embodied in critical reviews and certain other noncommercial uses permitted by copyright law. For permission requests, write to the publisher, addressed "Attention: Permissions Coordinator," at the address below.

J Merrill Publishing, Inc.
434 Hillpine Drive
Columbus, OH 43207
www.JMerrill.pub

Library of Congress Control Number: 2021921964
ISBN-13: 978-1-954414-29-7 (Paperback)
ISBN-13: 978-1-954414-28-0 (eBook)

Book Title: The Journey
Author: Rosetta Perry
Cover Artwork: germancreative

I dedicate this book in loving memory of my mother, Mrs. Julia Perry. My mom went to be with the Lord in heaven in May of 2005. I really do miss her, but I feel her love. She supported me in all my endeavors.

I am so grateful that my mom showed by example how to be a strong woman of God.

Thank you, mom, for praying for me to be all God intended for me to be.

CONTENTS

Foreword	ix
Introduction	xv

1. The Great I Am — 1
   Receiving Instructions
2. I Surrender — 5
   Your Will Be Done, Lord
3. I've Got An Angel — 9
   Protection All Around
4. Abundant Life — 15
   God Will Provide
5. Lord, I Bless Your Name — 21
   Worship is Essential
6. Jesus the Same — 27
   Faithful and True to His Word
7. I Am A Winner — 31
   You Already Have the Victory
8. My God's Good Pleasure — 37
   Conforming to His Desires
9. Smack Dab in The Middle — 41
   Right Place, Right Time
10. Trust God — 45
    Obedience Over Fear
11. He Told Me To Praise Him — 53
    Time to Sing, Shout, and Dance

Acknowledgments 57
About the Author 59

FOREWORD

The first song I can remember hearing was called "Zoom" by the group, The Commodores. Sure, I had listened to music before I was ten, but this song changed me. I was cleaning my room as my mother had instructed, and I wanted to listen to some music while I cleaned. When I heard that song, I stopped what I was doing, laid on my bed, closed my eyes, and went to a place I had never been before. Until that point in my short life, I had no idea that music could transport a person to another place and time. It was right then and there that I knew that I wanted to create music. Not just music that had a beat, or sounded good, or made people dance, but music that transported (and transformed) the listener. From that moment, I did not just listen to music; I heard it. When my mom played her music, I heard what the Mighty Clouds of Joy were asking when they sang, "If God is dead, what makes the flowers bloom?" I understood the conviction Mahalia Jackson possessed when she sang, "I believe above a storm the smallest prayer can still be heard."

I soon realized that music is not created. It is discovered. Many artists try to make music. Sure, they can get people to dance or sing along to their catchy melody, but that listener moves on unchanged once the song is over. But when music is discovered, a listener must pause, take note, and contemplate what they just heard. The lyrics, the melody, the beat, the chord changes, the combination of notes, the contrast of instruments, the vocal harmonies all contribute to an experience that takes you on a journey. A journey is something that suggests a passage from one place to another. When you go on a journey, you arrive at a completely different destination from where you started. Music that is discovered will do that very thing for the listener. Proverbs 25:2 says, "It is God's privilege to conceal things and the king's privilege to discover them. (NLT)"

When I first met Rosetta Perry, I knew she was both an explorer and a storyteller even before I heard her sing. She was a person who would go on a quest and discover great treasure, then bring it back for people to enjoy and share the story of her adventure. On one occasion, she and I were discussing faith, and I made the statement, "hope is faith." Rosetta was quick to correct me and even gave me a little booklet explaining the difference. However, she would not be satisfied by simply disagreeing with me. Instead, she took me on a journey of discovery. Discovery: This is what you will experience as you read this book and listen to the music of Rosetta's Journey.

When Rosetta and I got together and began discussing the project, I wanted to both hear the melodies and understand the lyrics. And as she sang each song, I immediately knew two things. One, much of the timing and format of the songs were unconventional, and two, this was more than just a collection of random songs. There was a story here to be told. So, it took some time, time to hear Rosetta, understand her revelation, and discover and extract the story of her journey. I sat down at my keyboard with only a piano sound and framed each song on the piano before searching for sounds and effects. I saw that this was a labor of love and an assignment for Rosetta. Therefore, I knew that the music had to both support and help frame the story. So, for example, when she sang, "tell them who sent you... the Great I Am," the music had to not only depict The Great I Am, but The Great I Am sending someone out with authority and power. So, I thought about every orchestra hit, string part, and chord structure.

I wanted to make sure that they elevated the words that were sung as well as the story that was being told. I had to discover the story behind the music before recording a note. And I believe that because we approached this process as discovery and creativity, we made, as Rosetta would say, Jello! So let me help you young musicians, singers, seekers of truth, storytellers, revolutionists, and influencers. Creating is overrated, but discovery is profound. I don't want to minimize the creativity in you. But when you see what Rosetta has discovered on her journey, you will know that you too must walk the path and cross rivers of discovery in order to create.

In this book, The Journey, Rosetta has allowed you to walk her path with her. She has invited you into a private place that will change you as much as it has changed her. From the moment you begin reading this book and listening to this project, you leave the mental place you're occupying and quickly become anxious to see where you'll end up. Rosetta is a visionary who allowed God to show her who He was, in "The Great I Am," show her who she is in "I Am a Winner," and show her His purpose for her in "He Told Me to Praise Him." This book will leave a lasting impact on you. So, once you've read it, Go Tell Them!

Michael Carter, Lead Pastor, The Life Church
Three-time author
Loving Jesus Transforming Lives,
Think on These Things,
I See You

INTRODUCTION

As a young girl, I was singing in the children's choir at church. I loved singing, and when I was older, I joined the youth choir and the young adult choir. I knew that my voice was a gift from God. I was blessed to lead songs with the choir and sing as a soloist as well. As a young adult, I realized the gifting and ability to write songs was always in me. It was released out of my spirit like a river when I was baptized with the Holy Spirit with the evidence of speaking in tongues. It was like breaking through a trapped door! The Lord inspired me to write songs, and it was so exciting and humbling to me. I would get song ideas from teachings I heard at church from my Pastor, David C. Forbes Jr., and from my personal time reading and meditating on the word. My Pastor would teach the word in such a powerful way that it was easy to understand. I would take lots of notes and read them over and over until I got a revelation of what God was saying to me. Then, during my quiet time with the Holy Spirit, I would begin to write songs from my heart. It was never difficult for me to write. The lyrics and the musical melodies just flowed out of my creative spirit. I could hear the music in my mind even though I had never played an instrument. I would use my tape recorder and sing the lyrics. Then I would make sounds to identify what instrument I heard in my head. I would beat on the kitchen table and tap on things to convey what I heard the best way I could. Every song was birthed with scripture references from the King James Version of the bible.

I met my first music producer Michael Carter through a friend at church. My Pastor, David C. Forbes Jr., said in a message that God orchestrates people, places, and circumstances to bring about his perfect will for our lives. I truly believe that!

Michael Carter was a man of God and an excellent anointed musician and experienced producer. He was able to take the tape recordings of what I heard musically in my head and create all the music for the first album. His skill and experience were exactly what I needed. As a new songwriter and recording artist full of faith and zeal, I certainly needed direction. It was important for me to work with someone who could feel my music and understand my personality and passion. I did not know much about the music industry or the business. But I knew the Holy Spirit connected me with a producer I could trust. Michael Carter was full of integrity and displayed a genuine relationship and love for Jesus Christ.

I love how the Lord would use personal parts of my life to create the story he wanted me to share with the world. I didn't know just how much my songs would bless and encourage people or even how it would encourage me! I just kept writing. I must have written 100 songs before I recorded my first album. Michael and I worked on this project for two years. The first single was recorded and sold on a cassette tape entitled "I've Got An Angel." Then the full project entitled "The

Journey" was recorded, produced, and released on a cassette tape in 1998. Wow, that sounds funny now since we have an entire generation who does not even know what a cassette tape is. After a few years, we released it on a CD. I remember mailing out demo tapes to different record labels. According to my producer, one label showed interest in my song "I've Got an Angel" as a possible choice for one of their artists to record. I was flattered, but I said no because I wanted to sing and record my own song. As a songwriter, I know that was a huge compliment.

I continued to stay focused on getting my music out, singing, and sharing it with the world. I was confident that God would orchestrate that for me. I was blessed to have some anointed friends that sang on the project.

They believed in my dream and supported me every step of the way. I thank God for Asa & Tanya Featherstone, Damien King, Derek Brown, and Detra Carter.

As an Independent artist with no label backing me financially, I had to trust God to provide the finances for studio time, promotions and distribution. We were walking by faith every step of the way. I also had great support from my church family at Columbus Christian Center Church. I continued to use my gift ministering at church as a Psalmist and choir member. It was very important to stay connected to my local church and my Pastor, my spiritual Father in ministry. My Pastor covered me in prayer and spoke into my life regularly. He recognized the anointing and the calling on my life and nurtured my gift. I am forever grateful for my awesome Pastors, David C. Forbes Jr., and Dr. Tracy Forbes.

We prayed about the title and the order in which the songs should be sequenced. When the Lord gave me the title "The Journey," he also helped me understand the purpose and the assignment I was chosen to do. God was calling me to do something I had never done before. The Lord was taking me on a personal journey with my music. A journey designed to mature me and cause me to walk in a greater level of faith as I delivered his message of hope, salvation, love, encouragement, and peace to the world. The messages of inspiration in each song are still just as relevant and needed today as it was 20 years ago!

God opened so many doors for me to sing my original songs from "The Journey" project. My songs were played on the local gospel radio station WVKO and The River 104.9. I was traveling and witnessing how my music blessed people.

In this book, I will share the scriptures and my personal stories that inspired me to write each song. My prayer is for you to be enlightened and encouraged as you go on your journey. I believe that my journey shall continue as I gain more insight and revelation through the timeless messages in the songs the Lord inspired me to write. So here we go!

God gave me the title "The Journey" from the scripture in Genesis 33:12 "And he said let us take our journey and let us go, and I will go before thee."

For me, this was my instruction from the Lord as he was calling me out to preach his gospel message to the world through my songs. It was clear that I was not alone: He said, "let us take our journey." He has places for me to go, and he is going with me, and he will go before me, leading the way because he knows where we are going. All I have to do is follow him and agree with blind faith. I had to walk by faith and not by sight, 2 Corinthians 5:7. I did not see everything in the natural, but I knew I could trust him to lead me in the spirit.

CHAPTER 1
THE GREAT I AM
RECEIVING INSTRUCTIONS

The first song on this faith walk is "The Great I Am" these scriptures inspired me.

> *And Moses said unto God, Behold, when I come unto the children of Israel, and shall say unto them, The God of your fathers hath sent me unto you; and they shall say to me, What is his name? what shall I say unto them? And God said unto Moses, I Am That I Am: and he said, Thus shalt thou say unto the children of Israel, I Am hath sent me unto you.*
>
> — Exodus 3:13-14 KJV

Now therefore go, and I will be with thy (your) mouth, and teach thee what thou shalt say.

— Exodus 4:12 KJV

I applied these scriptures to myself, and I made them personal. I said, Rosetta, just as I instructed Moses, I am instructing you. I will give you the words to say, to write, and to sing.

THE GREAT I AM

Intro
Go tell them, Won't you go tell them? Go tell them, Won't you go tell them?

Verse
Sing of my goodness, Sing of my praises Sing of my honor, glory and power

Chorus
I'm sending you out (go tell them)
I'm sending you out (won't you go tell them)
I'm sending you out (go tell them)
I'm sending you out (won't you go tell them)

Verse
Tell them I'm Alpha and Omega
Tell them I come, I come to save them I can change them, with my power
I'll give them peace, peace that surpasses all earthly understanding
Peace and joy that ...

Adlib

(Peace and joy that no man can give... peace and joy that no man can give)

Verse
I will protect them and give them shelter. I'll spread my wings as a cover
I'll bring them out of the raging storms, the storms of life, pain, and problems
I can renew their minds from all shame and confusion
OHHHHHH... I'm gonna bring them out

Vamp
Tell them who sent you
The Great I Am, The Great I Am, The Almighty God,
The Everlasting Father, The Prince of Peace The Royal Majesty, The Great I Am, The Great I am
The Lord of Lords, the Great Jehovah The Great Provider, The Rock of Ages
The Great I Am, The Great I Am, The Great I Am!

CHAPTER 2

I SURRENDER

YOUR WILL BE DONE, LORD

The next song is "I Surrender" The following scriptures inspired me.

> *He said I am the voice of one crying in the wilderness, making straight the way of the Lord, as said by the Prophet Esaias.*
>
> — JOHN 1:23

> *And he said unto them, go Ye into all the world, and preach the gospel to every creature.*
>
> — MARK 16:15

...whatsoever he sayeth unto you do it.

— JOHN 2:5B

As I wrote this song, I knew that I had to surrender myself to the Lord in every way, period. My life could no longer be about what I wanted; it had to be about what God wanted for my life. His will be done in me and through me. I admit that my decision was not always easy to carry out. There were so many occasions when I wanted to hang out with my friends and do what I wanted to do. I am sure you understand that my decision to go where the Lord was leading me was not always popular or fun, especially when everyone did not understand my "Journey." Still, it was always rewarding when I was obedient.

> I am crucified with Christ nevertheless I live; yet not I, but Christ lives in me, and the life which I now live in the flesh I live by the faith of the son of God who loved me and gave himself for me.
>
> — GALATIANS 2:20

I Surrender

Intro
I surrender my everything to you
I surrender my all and all to you   2x

Verse
I give my life to you, Lord
Use me as you will
I deny myself so that you can have my very best
Use me as you will

Chorus
I surrender my everything to you
I surrender my all and all to you

Verse
This life that I now live is not my own Christ lives is me
He made a human sacrifice one day for me on Calvary He died for me He set me free This life is not my own, this life is not my own

Verse
I know there is a place for me

Where the people are bound, and they need to be set free
I'll share my testimony. I'll give God the Glory
I surrender

Vamp
I'll go wherever you send me
I'll move when the spirit is moving
As you lead me, I will follow. Yes, I'll go

CHAPTER 3

I'VE GOT AN ANGEL
PROTECTION ALL AROUND

For he shall give his Angels charge over me, to keep me safe in all my ways.

— PSALM 91:11

Bless the Lord Ye his Angels that Excel in strength, that do his commandments, hearkening unto the voice of his word.

— PSALM 103:20

I believe that God knew there would be plenty of times to face fear and possible danger on this journey. Even after we say yes, there will be days when you may feel alone, but God reminded me about the Angels assigned to protect me.

Angels are very real, very powerful, and very capable of protecting me. I can honestly say that God is faithful. During difficult times in my life, I was able to see my Angels guarding and protecting me. One late night after work, I drove up to my townhouse. I parked the car in front of my front door. I could see two very large angels on either side of my door. In amazement, I sat in the car looking. I did not sense or feel afraid, so I got out and went to my door, and they did not move or speak. The angels were very large, very tall, and very strong.

I remember their faces were not visible to me. They were warriors on guard. I was assured by the Holy Spirit that God allowed me to see them as a reminder that I was protected. I felt an overwhelming sense of peace; I knew beyond a shadow of a doubt that he was always with me and I was safe. This was significant because there were times when I came home and found my front door open. There were items stolen from my home. My neighbors shared on several occasions that their homes had been broken into, and items were also stolen. Several years later, due to my friend who knew my story, I was featured on a television series with the news anchor Cabot Rae on WCMH channel 4. He was doing a series about people who had encountered angels.

I was able to tell my story, and sing my song and give God all the glory. This was another example of God orchestrating people, places, and circumstances to bring about his perfect will in my life. I am so blessed! I have seen angels in church during our worship service as well. When I was injured on my job and had to keep working, angels appeared to minister strength to me. They reminded me that God could see what I was going through, and help was available. I knew that I would make it. I had to endure the hard times like a soldier! God provided a way of escape for me to leave that job. I received money from the injury I had on the job and could finance my music project. The Journey was not always easy, but it was always worth it!

I've Got An Angel

Verse
So many people are living in fear,
afraid to leave their own homes
Afraid to walk in the park with their kids
There's mass destruction,
so much evil in the land
And it's all because of Satan's plan
But I've come to tell you don't be afraid
Being a prisoner to your own home
Is not God's way

Chorus
I've got an angel walking beside me, Clearing the
path in front of me, Watching my back behind me
And his only job is to protect and to serve me, and
He moves on my command
when He hears me – hears me Speaking the word
Quoting the word of Jesus, I'm not afraid – no –
I'm not afraid because I've got an angel walking
beside me, Clearing the path in front of me
Watching my back behind me
And his only job is to protect and to serve me, And
He moves on my command
when He hears me – hears me

Adlib
When I'm all alone, and I have someplace to go,
I'm not afraid because God's word says in Psalm
91:11 – for He shall give his angels charge over me
to keep me in all my ways:

Vamp
He is watching me, Angel watching me, He is
watching me

He's watching me, He's clearing the pathway I take
Him everywhere I go, He protects me There's
never any danger,
He's always watching me
Though I walk through the valley of the shadow of
death, I fear no evil because thy rod and thy staff
they comfort me – Thou preparest a place for me
in the presence of my enemy –
Oh yes, He does
I'm not afraid, no, no, no, no

He is watching me, Angel watching me, He is
watching me

CHAPTER 4
ABUNDANT LIFE
GOD WILL PROVIDE

but seek ye first the Kingdom of God and his righteousness and all these things shall be added unto you.

— MATTHEW 6:33

Ask and it shall be given you, seek and ye shall find, knock and it shall be opened unto you.

— MATTHEW 7:7

> *The thief cometh not but for to steal and to kill and to destroy: I am come that they might have life and that they might have it more abundantly*
>
> — JOHN 10: 10

As long as we live on this earth, we have needs. We need money for the bare necessities in life: rent or mortgage, Lights and electricity, and gas for warmth and cooking. We need shelter, food, and clothing for ourselves and our families. God's message to me was clear. I have to trust and depend on Him, my father, to provide because he already knows what we need. I learned that I needed to do what I could in my own strength by working for seed (money), but not to ever worry about my needs being met. God has a better plan for his children to live by, called abundant life. This is how he wants us to live. Simply trust him in all things, and he will multiply our seed sown in more ways than we could ever imagine.

On my journey, I have seen God cause money and favor to come to me as I obeyed his command and trusted and believed that he would always take care of me. He always made a way. This song calls us to live a higher life resting in his plan and provision no matter what you're facing, always seek God for answers and direction, and always keep God first. Do not worry! Take no thought! Trust him and be at peace as you expect him to come through.

To fulfill what God instructs me to do on the earth, it takes money, and God knows that. So I say: "it's the vision and assignment that you gave me, Lord, so you have to pay for it. Thank you, Father!"

Abundant life

Intro
Are you livin'? Are you livin'?

Verse
He said ask, and it will be given to you He said seek, and you will find
Knock, and the door will be open to you. There's no limit to what God can do

Chorus
Are you living the abundant life? The one that God promised to you Are you living the abundant life? The one that God promised to you

Verse
I know these things that you want to have in this life
And there's things that God wants you to have
Instead of worrying about how you're gonna get em, Just do what He says – yeah

Seek first the kingdom of God and his righteousness

And all these things will be added to you. There's no limit to what God can do

CHAPTER 5

LORD, I BLESS YOUR NAME

WORSHIP IS ESSENTIAL

The next song Lord I Bless Your Name, is all about worship. I could not survive on my Journey without taking time daily to tell God how much I needed him and loved him. Worship is like spiritual rejuvenation for my mind, body, and soul. This is a reminder for us all. While we are busy doing God's will and working in the kingdom, we must always worship the Lord of Lord's, the King of King's, in good times and bad times. He is worthy of all honor and all praise. I must admit there were times when I was not sure if I was making a difference with my music. I felt empty and unfulfilled at times, even though I was doing what God called me to do. Finally, I realized that I needed to put everything aside and just get in the presence of the Lord. I needed to refuel and replenish my soul. Sometimes we give of ourselves ministering to others. We forget to stop and take time to allow the Holy Spirit to minister to us. Worship is what I needed. During those times, the Lord would give me songs. Some were just for him, and this is one that he gave me to share with you.

The scriptures that inspired me to write this song are:

> *Oh come let us worship and bow down; Let us kneel before the Lord our maker.*
>
> — PSALMS 95:6

> *Enter into his gates with thanksgiving, and into his courts with praise: be thankful unto him, and bless his name.*
>
> — PSALMS 100:4

Exalt ye the Lord our God, and worship at his footstool; for he is holy.

— Psalms 99:5

Lord, I Bless Your Name

Chorus
Lord, I bless your name
Lord, I praise your name
Lord, I give you honor today

Verse
I exalt your holy name
I lift my hands, and I give you praise
 I bow down before you, Lord
I extol your name
You are worthy of all my praise

Chorus
Lord, I bless your name
Lord, I praise your name
Lord, I give you honor today

Verse
I will enter your gates
With thanksgiving and honor, I'll praise your name. With my whole heart, I will bless you, Lord
I'll lift my voice and sing your praise

Chorus
Lord, I bless your name
Lord, I praise your name
Lord, I give you honor today

Verse
I exalt your holy name
I lift my hands, and I give you praise. I will magnify your holy name
You're worthy Lord, you're worthy to be praised. I exalt your holy name

CHAPTER 6

JESUS THE SAME
FAITHFUL AND TRUE TO HIS WORD

As my Journey continued, I was encouraged to find that no matter what happened along the way, Jesus never changed. People will change around you all the time. It is heartbreaking sometimes when you put your trust in people. We try to understand what happened, and we think maybe it was something I did or said. The truth of the matter is people are not flawless. Sometimes they have good intentions, and sometimes they do not. My mom called them "Fairweather friends," you know the ones that stick close to you when things are going well for them as they benefit from riding on your coattails. I learned that not everyone could handle your success or your passion for living to please God. Once I accepted that truth and put all my focus on the one who would never change, life was much better for me. Knowing that his love for me will never change and that he is faithful and true to his word provided fuel for me to keep going.

The scriptures that inspired me to write this song, "Jesus The Same," are:

> *Every good gift and every perfect gift is from above and cometh down from the Father of lights with whom is no variableness, neither shadow of turning.*
>
> — JAMES 1:17

> *Jesus Christ the same, yesterday, today and forever.*
>
> — HEBREWS 13:8

Jesus The Same

Intro
Jesus the same today As He was back then
He never changes
He is faithful and true

Jesus the same today As He was back then,
And He will do for you
What He said He will do

Verse
From the beginning He was, Until now He is And tomorrow He will always be
In Him, there is no changing, No shadow of turning
As He is, He shall always remain

Verse
From the beginning, He was
Until now He is, And tomorrow He will always be
In Him, there is no changing, No shadow of turning
As He is, He shall always remain

Chorus
Shoo-be doop – shoo-be-doop
Shoo-be doop – shoo-be-doop – ahhhh

Chorus
Jesus will not change. You can depend on Him
He will do for you what He said He will do

He is the same today as He was yesterday. He will do for you what He said He will do

Verse
Just hold on to God's unchanging hand
He's the one, He's the one you can depend on
Just hold on He will do what He said He would do

Vamp
And remember that He wants you to know that He loves you so

Shoo-be doop – shoo-be-doop
Shoo-be doop – shoo-be-doop

CHAPTER 7

I AM A WINNER

YOU ALREADY HAVE THE VICTORY

Well, it was time for a wake-up call. Who said being a Christian, a believer, a follower of Jesus Christ would be easy? Whoever said this was misinformed. If you live long enough, you will face challenges and difficult situations. Some are the results of our sins and bad life choices. Some are the results of others' sins and bad decisions. Some things are just out of our control. Have you read about all the challenges the disciples had following Jesus? Doing the will of God gets rough sometimes. Salvation does not make you exempt from real-life challenges. There were times when I found myself questioning God, saying, why is this happening to me? I knew it was time for reinforcement from the word of God. The Lord had me write this song, "I Am A Winner," as a reminder of who we are in Christ Jesus! Although we have challenges like unbelievers, we should not respond the same. We handle it according to the word of God, our script or blueprint for the life of a true disciple of Jesus Christ. The following scriptures inspired me:

> *For whatsoever is born of God overcometh the world: and this is the victory that overcometh the world, even our faith. Who is he that overcometh the world, but he that believeth that Jesus is the Son of God?*
>
> — I JOHN 5: 4-5

> *I can do all things through Christ which strengtheneth me.*
>
> — PHILIPPIANS 4:13

These things I have spoken unto you, that in me ye might have peace. In the world you shall have tribulation: but be of good cheer I have overcome the world.

— JOHN 16: 33

No, in all these things we are more than conquerors through him that loved us.

— ROMANS 8:37

I Am A Winner

Intro - Spoken
Jesus said in this world you would have tribulation, but be of good cheer, I have overcome the world, For who is He that overcometh the world, it is He that believeth that Jesus is the Son of God!

Chorus
I am a winner – More than a conqueror, Greater is He that is in me
I am a winner – More than a conqueror, Greater is He that is in me
Than He that is in the world

Verse
Jesus said I have already overcome the world
So that you could live Not just barely getting by
But I want you to live a full life, A full and abundant life

Verse
Jesus said I have already made a way for you
All my promises are true

There is nothing that you cannot do. Trust me and believe

Special Chorus
I can do all things
Because Christ strengthens me, I can do all things
Because greater is He that is in me
Oooo oooo ooooo I am a winner, more than a conqueror greater is he that is in me

CHAPTER 8

MY GOD'S GOOD PLEASURE

CONFORMING TO HIS DESIRES

On my Journey, I learned so many lessons about putting God's purpose for my life first. I knew that my desires must line up with the desires that He put in my heart. I heard a man of God say, "When what is important to God is important to you, then what is important to you becomes important to God." It is very common for us to dream big dreams and desire great things for ourselves and our families. I realized that every dream we come up with is not from God. What we want is not always what God wants for us. He knows what we really need to succeed. But we sometimes forget to check in with the master planner who designed our lives from the end to the beginning. The more time I spent with the Lord, the more my heart's desires began to conform to his will and purpose for my life. I was inspired to write the song "My God's Good Pleasure," and the scriptures that inspired me are:

> *Delight thyself also in the Lord, and he shall give thee the desires of thine heart. Commit thy way unto the Lord; trust also in him, and he shall bring it to pass.*
>
> — Psalms 37:4-5

My God's Good Pleasure

Chorus
It is my God's good pleasure to give you the desires of your Heart
It is my God's good pleasure to give you the desires of your Heart
To give you the desires, to give you the desires, to give you the desires of your Heart

Verse
Delight yourself in the Lord, Commit thy ways unto Him
Humble yourselves in the sight of the Lord And be determined to do His will

Chorus
It is my God's good pleasure to give you the desires of your Heart
It is my God's good pleasure to give you the desires of your Heart
To give you the desires, to give you the desires, to give you the desires of your Heart

Verse
Bless the Lord at all times,
His praise shall continually be in your mouth
Exalt his name up high in all the earth Yield to his Spirit and do his will

Chorus
It is my God's good pleasure to give you the desires of your Heart
It is my God's good pleasure
To give you the desires, to give you the desires, to give you the desires of your Heart To give you the desires, to give you the desires, to give you the desires of your Heart

Vamp
To give you the desires, to give you the desires, to give you the desires of your Heart

CHAPTER 9

SMACK DAB IN THE MIDDLE

RIGHT PLACE, RIGHT TIME

Despite all the challenges I faced while working on this project, I knew that I was exactly where I was supposed to be on my Journey. I could see the hand of God orchestrating my life. I was having more fun than I ever imagined I would have. It did not matter how many hours I worked in the studio and at home rehearsing parts and perfecting the songs. It does not feel like work when you are doing what you were called to do pertaining to your purpose. Because of the level of peace and joy in my life, I wrote this song, "Smack Dab in the Middle." When we were rehearsing this song at my home, the spirit of laughter would fall on us every time. When it was time to record in the studio, the same thing happened. We recorded the laughter so everyone could hear it and hopefully have the same encounter as we all did. We did not plan it, but we figured the Holy Spirit wanted to demonstrate what was available to all who would hear this song. I was certainly happy about where I was in the middle of God's will. The scriptures that inspired me are:

Wherefore be ye not unwise, but understanding what the will of the Lord is.

— EPHESIANS 5:17

Jesus saith unto them, my meat is to do the will of him that sent me, and to finish his work.

— JOHN 4:34

Smack Dab In The Middle

Verse
I look around and what I see are people fighting in the streets'
I see destruction everywhere – so many people in despair
The one thing that puzzles me is why people live a life of defeat
I know that in my home we trust God and believe his word
We read the bible, and we pray every day
We live in peace and harmony in every way
Because we're

Chorus
Smack dab in the middle of God's will,
Smack dab in the middle of God's will
I wanna be in the middle, yes,
In the middle of God's will
Smack dab in the middle of God's will
Smack dab in the middle

Special Verse
In the middle of God's will
There is joy (smack dab in the middle)

There is love, (smack dab in the middle)
There is peace (smack dab in the middle)
There is hope (smack dab in the middle)

I wanna be in the middle, yes in the middle of God's will

Chorus
Smack dab in the middle of God's will, Smack dab in the middle (repeat)

Vamp
I Want to be in the middle of God's will. I like to stay – in His will
I like the peace that I feel in his will; I like the joy when I'm in his will, So much love when I'm in his will
I need to be in my God's will; I'm gonna stay in his will
Smack dab in the middle (repeat)

CHAPTER 10

TRUST GOD
OBEDIENCE OVER FEAR

While on my Journey, the Lord was maturing me in the area of trust. Walking with the Lord requires growth. He is always calling us higher. My time of testing had arrived. This next song was birthed from a personal battle I was having with fear and obedience. Out of all the songs I wrote on this project, this one is closest to my heart. The scriptures that inspired me and gave me courage became my favorite scriptures:

Trust in the Lord with all thine heart, and lean not unto thine own understanding. In all thy ways acknowledge him and he shall direct thy paths.

— PROVERBS 3: 5-6

Howbeit when the Spirit of truth has come, he will guide you into all truth: for he shall not speak of himself, but whatsoever he shall hear, that shall he speak: and he will show you things to come.

— JOHN 16: 13

Let us go over unto the other side of the lake. And they launched forth.

— LUKE 8: 22(B)

Now unto him that is able to do exceeding abundantly above all that we ask or think, according to the power that worketh in us.

— EPHESIANS 3:20

I can remember this situation just like it was yesterday. There was a gentleman that had been a part of my life for many years. We met in college, and I fell head over heels for him. We developed a very close bond and spent many years partying and singing and traveling together. Although we loved each other, the relationship never evolved into the kind of committed romantic relationship I desired. As far as I was concerned, he was the one! But after years of frustration and unanswered questions, feeling rejected and let down, I moved on. Even through future relationships, two marriage proposals, I never truly got him out of my system. I still considered him a friend, but we did not stay in touch as much.

Well, fast forward several years, we reconnected as brothers and sisters in Christ. We both had rededicated our lives to Christ and were focused on living for God and his purpose for our individual lives. So now God was orchestrating things in our lives to do kingdom work together as ministry partners. God would show me visions of us working together. We would pray about it and just wait on God to move on our behalf. He did, and the projects we did were blessed. So many people were blessed, and God was glorified. The

Lord would speak to him about supporting my songwriting and encouraging me along the way. So I started thinking, maybe we are supposed to be together now since God orchestrated all these things for us to work side by side. So as we grew closer in our brother and sister in Christ friendship, I started to develop romantic feelings and thoughts of a possible God-built marriage. But I was afraid to say anything to him because I did not want to mess up what we had as friends. It eventually became a stressful situation for me, not knowing what he was thinking or feeling about me. So I guess the Lord was tired of seeing me like this. He spoke to me in my spirit and said to talk to him about it and ask him his thoughts.

I was petrified! I did not want to rock the boat. I did not want to look or sound foolish. I did not want to feel rejected again. So I struggled for weeks battling with the Holy Spirit, not doing what he said, and I was losing the battle. The Holy Spirit would not let me rest or be in peace until I obeyed his instruction. He kept telling me to trust him. So after procrastinating for quite a while, I could not take it anymore. This gripping fear of the unknown was hindering me from moving forward with my relationship with God. So, with fear and literal trembling, I made the phone call. I did exactly what the Holy Spirit told me to do. We talked about it, and he said he had been wondering if we were supposed to be more than friends because of our strong connection. So after he prayed about it, we both accepted that we were to remain brother and sister in Christ. There was such a beautiful holy peace that flooded my soul. All the fear was gone! I did not feel rejected at all! I had been set free from fear gripping bondage! The Holy Spirit wanted us both to be free. We are still friends, and we continue to encourage and support each other in the things God has called us to do.

God needed me to pass this test. He was teaching me how to trust him in every situation, especially those involving my heart. He showed me that there were so many more things he had planned for me. I could not allow myself to be distracted from the purpose God was calling me to. So, letting go of something in the natural was hard to do, but the reward for my obedience was a powerful song. It does not matter what situation you're facing. Just "Trust God" and obey.

Trust God

Verse
If you're faced with a situation
That requires you to lay it on the line
To tell the truth about your feelings and emotions
The fear of rejection may rise up inside
You may hear a load of Satan's lies
But don't be afraid; go ahead, be strong,
God will not leave you alone
When He's leading you to tell the truth, obedience
must override all doubt and fear
He only wants to take you higher

Chorus
Trust God be real be true God will take care of you
Trust God be real be true God will take care of you

Verse
Come let us go to the other side
I'll show you the secret things.
The truth will make you free
It feels so good to be free
It feels so good to be free

Verse
He wants to take you higher Come let us go to the other side
My peace I give to you
I'll show you things to come. Follow my lead

Verse
So much more of me that I want you to see
I want to take you to places you have never dreamed
You need to trust me; you need to believe
I only want to take you higher; lock your wings and fly with me

You can live in perfect peace, I'll never leave you, I won't forsake you
I love you and I only – I only want to bless you
I will do exceeding, abundantly above all that you could ever ask or think

Vamp
The best is yet to come, but you've got to believe
I only want to take you higher; lock your wings
I only want to take you higher; lock your wings and fly with me

CHAPTER 11

HE TOLD ME TO PRAISE HIM

TIME TO SING, SHOUT, AND DANCE

God brought me a mighty long way on my Journey. All that is left to do now is to praise him. So this last song on this project is "He Told Me To Praise Him."

I love reading the book of Psalms, and these scriptures inspired me:

> Upon an instrument of ten strings, and upon the psaltery; upon the harp with a solemn sound, praise him.
>
> — Psalms 92:3

> I will sing unto the Lord as long as I live: I will sing praise to my God while I have my being.
>
> — Psalms 104:33

I remember when the Lord dropped this song in my spirit. I was dancing and singing in the driveway. This song reminds us that we should never stop praising the Lord God almighty for who he is and for all he has done! One of my friends shared that while her son was locked up in jail, he kept singing this song until he was released. He said it kept him encouraged. His testimony reminded me of Paul and Silas, who were also locked in jail, and they sang praises until the angels came and set them free. I praise God for choosing me to be an instrument of praise for him. I will forever use my voice to sing his praises wherever this Journey leads me. I will sing praises on the mountain top and in the valley low. May my praise encourage others to do the same!

He Told Me To Praise Him

Verse
He told me to bless his name,
He told me to praise Him,
He told me to bless his name Oh oh oh,

Chorus
I'm gonna praise Him,
I'm gonna bless his name,
I'm gonna praise Him,
I'm gonna bless his name

Verse
How ya gonna praise Him
I'm gonna praise Him on the timbrel and the harp
I'm gonna praise Him in the dance
I'm gonna praise Him on the drum
I'm gonna praise Him with my whole Heart

How ya gonna praise Him
I'm gonna praise Him on the timbrel and the harp
I'm gonna praise Him with the dance. I'm gonna praise Him in my testimony Of the things that He has done

Verse
Why, Why ya gonna praise Him?
He said He'd bless me
if I favor his Righteous cause
And I'm looking for a blessing in return
He will bless me if I favor
He'll bless those who favor his righteous cause

Vamp
Show me how you praise him
Praise him praise him praise him (repeat)

ACKNOWLEDGMENTS

To my entire Perry, Thomas, Fenderson family, My Pastors David and Tracy Forbes, my Columbus Christian Center Church family, my producer Michael Carter and to all my friends near and far who pushed me to complete this book.

ABOUT THE AUTHOR

Rosetta Perry was born and raised in Youngstown, Ohio. She grew up in a loving Christian home and knew that she loved singing and acting, and making people laugh at an early age. Rosetta is the youngest sibling; she has a brother and a sister. She has one son and three grandsons. After graduation from her Alma Mater, Youngstown State University, she relocated to Columbus, Ohio, pursuing her passion for singing and acting.

Rosetta has acted on many stages around the country with Words 2 Life Drama Ministry and Stew Jacks Entertainment. She also performed in the 2014 Washington DC Urban Theater Festival. In addition, she has recorded two Gospel CDs and one live Comedy CD.

- The Journey
- It's All About Love, Volume 1;

Rosetta loves people and encourages them to live life to the fullest! She believes in the ministry of laughter and enjoys doing clean stand-up comedy as a professional comedian. She also performs her Comedic One Woman Show entitled "You Just Need to Laugh," featuring her beloved character Bonnie Mae Ray Lewis. "The oldest reigning beauty queen" from the fictional town of YU, Georgia.

Rosetta was inspired to create this character through her mother's funny stories about growing up in the South on a farm with 13 siblings and strict family values. She performs at family reunions, church events, conferences, and corporate events.

Rosetta has been a regular comedian for the past 8 years at the Funny Bone Comedy Club in Easton Town Center (Columbus, OH) with XTreme Gospel Comedy.

Rosetta acted in her first featured film released in July 2017 entitled Holy Hustle. Produced by Walk on Water Productions with Mark Cummings.

She is the founder of Rosetta Perry Productions LLC.

She is a proud 2016 graduate of Increase Community Development Corporation for the Small Business Entrepreneur. She also is a proud 2017 graduate from the Lincoln Theatre Expand Your Horizons Incubation Program. Rosetta has been a featured comedy host on Joy WVKO and a featured guest on the Trinity Broadcasting Network in 2015, 2016, 2017. She is on a mission from God to spread joy and laughter worldwide by any clean means necessary.

Contact Information:
(614) 288-9056
rosettaloves2laugh@gmail.com

facebook.com/rosetta.perry.1

www.ingramcontent.com/pod-product-compliance
Lightning Source LLC
Chambersburg PA
CBHW071509070526
44578CB00001B/482